SAVE ME
softly

Zoya kanni

BLUEROSE PUBLISHERS
India | U.K.

Copyright © Zoya Kanni 2025

All rights reserved by author. No part of this publication may be reproduced, stored in a retrieval system or transmitted in any form or by any means, electronic, mechanical, photocopying, recording or otherwise, without the prior permission of the author. Although every precaution has been taken to verify the accuracy of the information contained herein, the publisher assumes no responsibility for any errors or omissions. No liability is assumed for damages that may result from the use of information contained within.

BlueRose Publishers takes no responsibility for any damages, losses, or liabilities that may arise from the use or misuse of the information, products, or services provided in this publication.

For permissions requests or inquiries regarding this publication, please contact:

BLUEROSE PUBLISHERS
www.BlueRoseONE.com
info@bluerosepublishers.com
+91 8882 898 898
+4407342408967

ISBN: 978-93-7018-673-6

Cover design: Yash Singhal
Typesetting: Namrata Saini

First Edition: April 2025

Dedication

This book is a reflection of the things I've always questioned, the things we do, the pressures we face and the silence that surrounds them.

It comes from the need to express the emotions and experiences that often go unnoticed. It's for the moments that are hard to put into words, the struggles that aren't often spoken about, and the feelings that don't always have a place to be shared.

This is for those who understand what it means to live with these questions, even when no answers seem to come.

Playlist
I love you
Billie Eilish
M.
Anil Emre Daldal
The one that got away
Katy Perry
The Night We met
Lord Huron
Driver's License
Oliva Rodrigo
Somewhere Only we know
Keane
Apocalypse
Cigarettes after sex
Co2
Parteek kuhad
Glided Lily
Cults
Tv
Billie Eilish
Ghost
Justin Bieber
Can't catch me now
Oliva Rodrigo
Rainy days
V
Heart Attack

Nothing's New
Rio Romeo
No one noticed
The Marias
Play date
Melanie Martinez
Rewrite The stars
James Arthur, Ann Marie
Cinnamon Girl
Lana Del Rey
Salvatore
Lana Del Rey
Still with you
Jungkook

"Love yourself enough to live,
But if you must fall,
Let it be in your own arms
No one else's to catch you,
No one else to blame."

Looking back at the missing pieces,
I wonder
Are they mine to reclaim,
Or just a part
I must not touch!

I miss my curly hair,
My blue haired doll,
And that old lemon tree
Things that stayed behind
While I kept moving forward.

I wonder what night whispers to the stars
Does it complain how late they come,
Or how they never stay

Contents

Where we were never meant to be 1

The art of being unseen 2

A gesture too far from mine 4

Where we once belonged 5

A battle that was never mine 6

Not the middle, not the beloved 8

The muted goodbye in the rain 10

Return to when they where here 12

Penning ghost of a friendship lost 13

A home i once knew 14

Love remains same maybe 15

A voice caged in his shadow 16

Love collects its debt in the quiet 18

Unheard, unhealed, unloved 20

Surrounded yet forgotten 22

Love graded and denied 23

The lemon tree still remembers 25

Burn my tongue and i will speak in flames 26

Hurting where the world won't see 29

Is this mine to keep? 32

What if he wears my father's face 33

A world where he never meets her	34
Orphean yearning	36
Eclipsed vow	38
The winter i forgot to feel	41
The hands that never held me	42
Lies kissex by your name	44
Dialects of the heart	46
What the past couldn't carry	48
Tears of a love long gone	49
Better the bear than a man	50
A history written in blood	51
Carving a blade to the bone	52
The life without a line	53
The art of being enough	54
The quite plea	55
The lost chronicle	56
Mend without peeling	57
The art of being patient	58
The weight of goodby	60
The love from thousand years ago	61

Where we were never meant to be

Cold water feels warm
When your hands are freezing
Like swans floating on frozen lakes,
Silent, their wings still.
There's no fight, no flight,
Just surrender to the ache,
A quiet acceptance of cold
They never thought to break.
They call it love,
But it's the kind that settles in cracks,
Slow and sharp,
Like water turning to ice
Beautiful, until it breaks you in half.
And they endure it,
Not knowing they were never broken,
Only misplaced
Hearts meant for sunlight,
Left to wither in the snow.

The art of being unseen

A story I tell, but it's never been told,
Whispers of connection, lost in the fold.
There are places where I should have been,
But the space beside them feels too thin.
The moments shared, but never mine,
Where laughter echoes, yet I don't shine.
Hands reach out, but never for me,
I watch as they weave their tapestry.
Not abandoned, not erased,
Just a shadow, fading without a trace.
The art lies in the quiet, untouched by the crowd
A presence that lingers but never too loud.
I'm the backdrop of lives I can't touch,
The words they share but never as much.
A fleeting glance a soft wave that fades,
In the space between thoughts where silence pervades.
I stand on the edge of the stories they tell,
A whisper lost in the louder yell.
I move through the world but I don't quite belong
A quiet hum, but never the song.
Not forgotten just overlooked
A chapter unspoken a page never booked

I'm there but not fully a hint in the air
A trace of existence that no one can spare
So here I remain unseen but not gone
Like a breath of wind or a soft silent dawn.
Lying in the grass where the world can't find
A piece of the universe, buried deep in the mind.

A gesture too far from mine

What is he doing, bringing flowers and chocolates,
I ask my mom, as if the answer is something I lack,
A gesture of care, a language of love,
Yet, the meaning escapes me, a question above.
Why do I feel like something's missing,
When it's just his smile, the kindness he's giving?
Is it the bloom or the sweet, tender bite,
That brings joy, but leaves me in fright?
I wonder what he's searching for in me,
What answer, what truth, will set us both free
The gifts, the words they're just a part
Of a language I don't yet understand in my heart

Where we once belonged

I sit at the end of the bus,
Each lurch a jolt, a whisper of us.
With every break, a flash of despair,
Everything I tried to hold isn't there.
Slipping through fingers like grains of sand,
Memories fading, unplanned, unmanned.
The hum of the wheels a quiet groan!
And I wonder where is my home?
Is it a place, a face?, a name?
A refuge that shields from the wind and flame?
Or is it the emptiness I carry inside,
The one place no one can ever reside?
I sit at the end of the bus, alone,
Searching for a home I've never known
It's not here, but maybe it's nowhere,
A weight that lingers, steady and bare.
Maybe it's not the person, but their presence,
A quiet pull, a steady essence.
Maybe it's not self-love that makes it a home,
But the doubts that settle when you're alone.
The fragile moments where fear takes its place,
And after it all the choice to embrace.
To hold the cracks, the sharp, the raw,
To find the truth within the flaw.
Perhaps home isn't found, but slowly made,
In the strength to stand where shadows fade.

A battle that was never mine

The Clock Hits 6
The clock hits 6, and I sit to think,
What is there about my family that I can fix?
Dad comes to mind—I hate my clothes,
And the wind outside, though it softly blows.
To my mom, it's pretty, the night's quiet frame,
But I see the wind, and it's never the same.
Covered in blood from the chaos last night,
And I wonder why did I think he could ever be right?
We move from house to house,
Running from what was once right.
The wind outside sharp and cold,
But the weight inside is still heavier.
I don't recognize the faces anymore,
Maybe I never did.
As time keeps moving,
We leave behind what we thought we knew.
The strawberry milkshake falls to the ground with my heart,
Just like I do every time I try to know what's about to start.
The rain falls softly, blending with the sea,
I've tried, but I could never be me.
Scratches all over my arms,
A mark of battles, invisible, but calm.
The pain is familiar, a dull, quiet throb,
A reminder of things I can't solve or stop.

The walls close in, but they never fall,
I'm stuck in a silence, lost in it all.
Trying to find something real, something true,
But it's hard to know me when I don't know you.
The bruises fade, but the memories stay,
In the corners of my mind, they'll never decay.
I reach for answers, but they slip like sand,
Grasping at nothing, trying to understand.
So I run and run for answers, my feet are numb,
Chasing after something, but it never comes.
The world keeps spinning, the questions grow wide,
But the truth feels distant, just out of sight.
Each step is heavy, but I keep on the chase,
Hoping for something that might show me grace.
The answers slip by, like sand through my hands,
And all I'm left with are the footprints in the sands.
I try to hold on, to grasp what is real,
But the harder I reach, the less I can feel.
Running for answers, but they're just out of sight,
I keep moving, though I'm losing the fight.

Not the middle, not the beloved

My voice trembled, yet I stood,
But her anger came, sharp as it could.
For speaking to him with my own mind,
She scolded me as if I'd crossed the line.
And then I wondered, in her weary eyes,
How many times had she swallowed her cries?
How often was silence her only shield,
Against battles she could never yield?
I loved the colour blue once, its depth serene,
Until it whispered of a childhood unseen.
Now it mocks me with every hue,
Dragging me back to the child I outgrew.
It's strange how love for a shade can fade,
When it ties you to a past you prayed away.
My life played out like a fleeting reel,
The reasons to move forward etched in steel.
Never to look back, never to stay,
Just carry the weight and drift away.
I wasn't the middle child, not quite in-between,
But never the beloved in the family scene.
My name, just a whisper in casual talk,
Forgotten when it mattered, a shadow to walk.
When they share pride, when they heal or divide,
I am the one left outside.
But in the quiet, I forge my own way,

A voice unbroken, no longer swayed.
In friends, I was always the one to speak,
To get caught, but at least it wasn't a cage.
Not 14 anymore, but still not the beloved,
Something's changed in me, something's evolved
I hate having taken care of those who never cared.
I hate that I stood by, while they took and took,
Never asking how I felt, never once a second look.
I was the one to patch wounds, to smooth the cracks,
But where were they when I needed that?
Now, I find it hard to play the part,
To be the one who always gives from the heart.
It's no longer a role I wish to fill,
I'm tired of empty promises, tired of the still.
I'm no longer that girl, with open arms,
No longer the one who shelters from harm.
The cage has broken, the silence grown loud,
And I stand alone, unapologetically proud.

The muted goodbye in the rain

The rain stops
As I'm speaking to you
On the other line.
My voice spills out,
Cracked,
Fragile like old glass,
Followed by a whimper.
The silence between us
Grows heavier,
Like the clouds that just passed,
Leaving behind
A damp chill
That clings to my chest.
I wonder if you hear the storm
In my voice,
The way it flutters,
The way it tries to hold on
To something slipping
Through the cracks.
No, I'm not crying.
But somewhere,
Between saving chocolate wrappers
And tying bows you never noticed,
I folded pieces of us
Into secret photographs,

Kept them in a corner
Of my mind I swore
You'd never see.
I captured moments
Like fireflies in jars,
Saving them for the last
As though there'd be a time
To look back.
But how foolish it feels now,
To wish for forever,
To think we'd be buried together,
Only to be left
Waiting for something to matter.
And if you wish to stay,
Stay like it's the last day.
But if you can't,
Don't leave a trace,
Let your absence be a quiet grace,
And vanish without a face.

Return to when they where here

My mom told me a story today,
Of sunlit afternoons and skies of grey,
She spoke of a backyard, quiet and wide,
Where her grandfather would sit by her side.
She'd bring him peaches, their sweetness shared,
A quiet bribe to keep him there.
With every bite, a tale would unfold,
Of fairies, of heroes, and kingdoms of gold.
His voice was a river, calm and deep,
Carrying her to lands she'd keep,
In her heart, where dreams would stay,
As he weaved magic in his gentle way.
She loved him not for the stories alone,
But for the warmth he always shone.
A bond of love, tender and true,
A timeless tale for me and you.

Penning ghost of a friendship lost

If in the next life I meet you again,
I'll remind you of how it all began
How we became friends, the laughter we shared,
The silly fights that showed how we cared.
I'll tell you how we used to hide each other's dolls,
Just to annoy, through giggles and calls.
And I'd tease you about your teeth, so bright,
Yet they made me smile, even in a fight.
But if in the next life, we never meet,
I'll fill the void with words bittersweet.
I'll write of longing, of a friend I once knew,
And how no one else could ever be you.
If a friend appears, I'd still pen the pain,
Of missing you in sunshine and rain.
Because no bond could ever compare,
To the one we had, beyond what's fair.
In lives apart, I'll still hold you near,
Through ink and memory, through love and tears.

A home I once knew

"Some things are meant to scatter,
To drift with wind unknown."
I wonder if it's the flowers,
Or us this world speaks of.
I think of how much of me
Has drifted away,
Just for the morning to come.
And if I do drift away,
Will I gather again, whole?
Or leave pieces behind,
Where the wind carries the stack?
And if somehow I do come back,
Will there be hands to hold?
Or only a shadow of warmth,
Familiar, yet not my own?

Love remains same maybe

Loving forever can't be wrong,
But maybe forever was never too strong.
You're slipping away, and I watch you drift,
Each memory of you becomes a heavy gift.
I've packed them gently, one by one,
Moments of us, of what we've become.
In a box named memories, tied with ribbons of green,
Pieces of a love that once felt right
I'll place it high on a quiet shelf,
A relic of you, and my old self.
I can't open it, and I can't forget,
But it feels lighter now without regret.
And as I leave it, I whisper goodbye,
To the echoes of you that linger inside.
For loving forever might not be wrong,
But holding on too tightly won't make me strong.

A voice caged in his shadow

I speak loud,
Loud for rights,
Loud for being a woman,
For my womanhood,
For all the voices silenced before me.

But when my father smiles
Across the dinner table,
I fall quiet.
Not out of fear,
Not out of doubt,
But because that smile feels like home,
A refuge I'd give anything to protect.

Yet sometimes, I sit back and wonder,
Would his smile fade
If his daughter spoke louder?
If I stood tall and said,
"I am a woman,
And I demand equality,
I demand respect."

Would he look at me with pride,
Or would disappointment cast a shadow?
Would he still smile and say,

"She is my daughter,"
Or would my voice
Feel too unfamiliar, too defiant?

I love him, I truly do.
But the question lingers:
Can I be both?
A fighter for my rights,
And his beloved child?
Or does my silence
Keep his world unshaken,
While mine trembles beneath it?

Love collects its debt in the quiet

He looks at me, "It's easy, isn't it?"
I glance at him and ask, "What?"
"Not putting effort, yet loving me."
I meet his gaze, a sigh slips free,
"It's not easy don't you see?
It's catching the weight in your silence,
Standing steady through your storms."
You think love asks for nothing back,
But it lingers in the space you lack
When your words turn sharp, your mind withdrawn,
Yet I stay, holding on.
It's in the nights when silence weighs,
When distance builds in quiet ways.
It's in the way you pull apart,
Leaving questions in my heart
It's not easy watching you drift,
Knowing I can't pull you back.
Love is harsh, yet still, I stay,
Through every storm, through every fray.
It's not easy fearing time will steal
The warmth I give, the love I feel
That one day, someone else will see
The parts of you reserved for me.
I love you, but not with ease,
It's holding on when you retreat.
It's fighting doubt, the weight, the war

And wondering if you'd fight as hard,
If love ever asked for more.

Unheard, Unhealed, Unloved

He stands tall, words sharp as knives,
Hiding behind pride, as if he's alive.
"Unworthy," he spits, a man so proud,
His voice loud, yet hollow, the silence loud.
What does he know of strength or grace,
When his every word is a hollow chase?
A man who tears, but never builds,
A man whose worth is defined by what he kills.
His power isn't in holding tight,
But in cutting down, hiding from light.
He thinks he's strong, thinks he's whole,
But inside, he's empty, a fractured soul.
He talks of respect but knows none,
His hands wield control, a life undone.
He'll never see, never understand,
That strength lies not in a clenched hand.
"Am I a good father?" he asks, voice weak,
But what he's done speaks louder than what he'll seek.
He wants answers, but he's blind to the truth,
A father who bruises is no father, that's proof.
His hands, they leave scars, they don't heal,
And his words, they cut, they never feel.
He asks, but the answer's already clear
A good father doesn't install fear.
He doesn't break, he doesn't destroy,

A man who loves doesn't wield his power as a toy.
He can ask all he wants, but it's too late,
For the answer's in the damage, the self-inflicted hate.
A good father doesn't hurt, he protects,
But he's too lost to see his own defects.

A man does not leave bruises
On the body he claims to love.
He doesn't twist, doesn't push, doesn't shove.
He doesn't use pain as a way to stay above.
His strength lies in kindness, in building, not breaking,
In actions that heal, never forsaking.
He doesn't wear love as a mask for control,
He doesn't use fear to secure his role.
Instead, he lets go of the grip he holds tight,
And builds with care, not with fright.
A man who loves doesn't leave a scar,
He creates a home, not a prison from afar.

Surrounded yet forgotten

I look over my friends, their laughter in bloom,
Talking of pastries, and the sports teacher's gloom.
Their voices weave stories, familiar and near,
Yet I sit in the silence, longing to hear.
I wish they'd turn, just once, my way,
To ask how I feel or what I'd say.
About the chocolate pastries they adore,
Or the jokes they've shared a hundred times before.
It's not the words that I truly miss,
But the space to belong in moments like this.
A quiet hope, a fragile plea
Will they ever glance and think of me?
Maybe I am in the wrong place,
A stranger seeking a fleeting embrace.
Their laughter feels distant, though it surrounds,
Like a song whose melody my heart confounds.
Or maybe silence was always mine to take,
A quiet companion, no noise to fake.
Perhaps my voice was never meant to be loud,
Just a whisper lost in the crowd.
But even in silence, I hope they'd see,
The quiet parts of who I could be.
Not just a shadow, not just a face
But a soul trying to leave a trace

Love Graded and denied

Maybe I've lost what Mom used to love me for,
And Dad doesn't smile at me anymore.
Aren't my grades enough to bring them pride?
Or have I failed where expectations reside?
I try so hard to be the one they need,
But their silence grows, like a growing weed.
Each mark, each score, feels like a plea,
A desperate cry for them to see me.
Am I not enough, beyond the test?
Is there no worth in all the rest?
Their laughter fades, their warmth feels cold,
And I'm left chasing love that feels so old.
Maybe it's me, or maybe it's time,
That makes their love feel harder to find.
But deep in my heart, I hope they'll see,
I'm more than the grades they're not all of me.
Maybe they'll notice I can sing better,
The notes I hold, the words I tether.
Maybe they'll hear the strength in my voice,
A melody shaped not by grades, but choice.
Maybe they'll notice how well I speak,
The passion I pour when my heart's at its peak.
Maybe my words will touch their core,
Will they see me, or ignore once more?
Or maybe they'll never, no matter how loud,

No matter how bright I stand in the crowd.
Perhaps their gaze is fixed on the past,
Where only perfection could ever last.
But still, I'll sing, and still, I'll speak,
For the love I crave, I'll continue to seek.
And even if they never see,
I'll learn to be enough for me.

The Lemon tree still remembers

I take those lemons from my favourite tree,
As I think about what went wrong.
No words come, no whispered sound,
But only regret and silence linger long.
The rain falls softly, as if it knows,
How deep the sorrow that nobody shows.
I grasp the roots, with hands that ache,
Hoping somehow, this pain will break.
But all I find is quiet still,
A void where words once filled.
I regret sharing my heart with you,
If I knew you wanted to hold both pieces too.
The bus stops silent at the gate,
And I wonder if it's too late
To undo the roads I've walked,
To silence the echo of the words we never talked.

Burn my tongue and I will speak in flames

Maybe It's Not Her
She was 13
When her mother asked her to hide
To hide what was bleeding,
To hide what she was going through,
To fold herself small enough
That no one could see what was changing.
She was 14
When her father said,
"Don't go outside at night."
The words felt like chains,
As if the darkness wasn't the sky,
But something waiting for her.
She was 16
When she felt uncomfortable in her own home,
Her skin shrinking under the weight
Of eyes that lingered too long,
Walls that whispered secrets
She wasn't meant to understand.
And she was 17
When she looked at herself in the mirror,
Hands trembling at her sides,
And asked
"Why am I a girl?

Is this a gift,
Or is it a question I'll never stop answering?"

Maybe it's not her.
Maybe it's the world.
Maybe it's the people who say,
Or maybe it's the people who do
The ones who commit sins
And then say,
"Women ask for sins."

Maybe it's the child,
Raised to believe his tears are weakness,
That softness isn't his to hold,
That manhood is a fortress of silence and steel.
But no one tells him
"Be a man,
Not to oppress or control,
But to protect, to lift,
To be a shelter when the storm comes."

Maybe it's the weight of tradition,
The invisible chains passed down like heirlooms,
Teaching girls to hide,
To lower their eyes,
To shrink their voices.

Maybe it's not her at all
Not her body, not her choices,
Not the way she walks,
Not the clothes she wears.
Maybe it's the world
That needs to learn how to heal,
How to unlearn its cruelty,
How to stop asking women
To carry the blame for sins
That were never theirs to begin with.

Hurting where the world won't see

I look over at my friend.
"It's been a long time," I say.
These words leave my mouth
Just before tears take hers
I don't need to ask.
Her silence is louder than any question.
She opens up, cracks in her voice,
Saying she hurts herself.
But her mom says it's for attention.
She looks at me and says she doesn't know why she does it,
But whenever she does it,
She hears a voice in her head.
It says she deserves it,
That this is the only way she can go for things.
So she does it,
And she hides it.
I beg her to come to therapy with me,
Maybe she'll heal, maybe she'll breathe,
Maybe she'll look forward to what's not underneath.
She says she'll be fine.
That she's always been fine with or without me.
And that's when it hits me.
I regret the moments I couldn't come for her.
I wish I could do something,

But right now, all I see is bruises on her skin
Bruises that tell a different story.
Her eyes, a lot different from what they used to be.
I don't think I...
I don't think the person I see is her.
It's not her. It could never be.
My face soaked with tears,
I try to ask her why she does it.
I realize there's a crack in my voice
Before I can finish the question.
She looks at me, her voice barely a whisper.
"I don't know.
Every time I do it,
I feel like I should.
Mom regrets having me.
And Dad doesn't have time.
And you left me."
And in that moment,
I wish I could go back
Back to when her laugh still felt like home,
To when I didn't have to ask

How much of herself did she sacrifice,
To feel she was enough, to shatter the ice?
She doesn't say another word.
The silence between us speaks volumes,
And in that moment, I feel the weight of her world
And I realize how little I truly knew.

Days slip by and I watch someone else do what she used to.
That's when it hits me.
Our worlds are fragile
To never let it happen again.
Like the tide washing over the shore,
Present and endless,
To see her breathe like the grass in the spring,
To see her stand tall like trees in the forest,
Strong, rooted, and alive.
Sometimes, things are left unsaid
But they're still worth hearing.

Is this mine to keep?

How do you know it's for you?
Does the sky bleed, or do the birds stop chirping?
Does God send a call, or do angels arrive at your table?

Do the stars rearrange, spelling your name?
Or does the wind whisper secrets, soft and untamed?
Is it a thunderous roar, a celestial decree,
Or just a stillness that roots you like a tree?

Perhaps it's none, no grand display,
Just a quiet knowing that finds its way.
No signs, no symbols, no heavenly cue,
Yet somehow, you feel it's meant for you.

But then a doubt touches your brain,
And you whisper, "No, it's not for me."
Yet, wasn't the pain the same refrain,
And still, you bore it silently?

You questioned the joy but embraced the ache,
Trusted the sorrow, let your heart break.
So why deny what feels so near,
When even pain found its way here?

What if he wears my father's face

How do I know he won't turn out like my dad?
I mean, I love my dad,
But if the universe did some magic,
And I were no longer his daughter,
I wouldn't want my mom to ever meet him.

I carry his love in my veins,
But also the scars he left unspoken.

So how do I know what's right or wrong,
When all I've done my life is hide,
Hide from the man I was supposed to love,
The one I never allowed close by my side.

I kept my distance, unsure of what to feel,
Afraid of what his love might bring,
Now I wonder if I've run so far,
That I no longer know how to feel anything.

A world where he never meets her

If I get another life,
I will spend it as my mother's shadow,
Watching her giggle, watching her achieve
The dreams she locked away with my childhood
makeup box.

I would watch her fall in love with a man
Who is nothing like my dad,
And I would make sure she never meets my father
I would watch her be cherished and loved,
Like never before
Her house will be filled with lilies,
Soft petals and fragrance that linger,
The calm of their beauty spreading through,
Her favourite books,

And her husband,
With some romcom hooks

And then, maybe,
I would sigh, and sigh again,
"Finally, my breaths aren't the reason
For all the wrongs."

Then, I would slowly fade away,
Letting her live,
Never trying to let her know
That I was the one she stayed for ,
Like blind to a cheating husband
She stayed with bruises for me , was never really fine
And a broken glass of wine.

Orphean yearning

You won't ever miss me the way I do,
His last words faded, cold but true.
I never told him, though he'd see
I couldn't miss him the way he missed me.
Not when I'm alone, but in the crowd,
His voice will echo, soft yet loud.
In sunlight's glow, in shadows deep,
He lingers there where parted lovers weep
I will miss him when I brush my hair,
When silence falls, he's always there.
I'll miss him when I sing our song,
When every note feels right and wrong.
I'll miss him when I see love bloom,
A tender spark in a crowded room.
I'll miss him in ways I'll never say,
In every night, in every day.

I will miss him when I have everything but him,
When the light feels full, but the edges dim.
I will miss him when time gives me space,
To replace his ghost, to forget his face.
I'll miss him when the cherry blossoms bloom,
When their petals dance, and they fill the room.
I'll miss him when the sunset tans my skin,
When the world feels calm, yet screams within.

I'll miss him in laughter, in quiet despair,
In the weight of moments we couldn't share.
I'll miss him when seasons rise and fade,
In every choice I've yet to have made.

Eclipsed vow

Why Aren't We Together? "You feel it, don't You?
The way we pull toward each other?" His voice cracks,
raw and full of everything he's been holding back.
"We're both here, aching for the same thing, so why
are we pretending it's not enough?"
I try to steady my breath, but his words hit like waves,
relentless.
He steps closer, the space between us shrinking, his
emotions spilling into the air.
"You love me," he says, softer now, but no less certain,
no less fierce. "And God, I'm so in love with you.
So why the hell are we still standing apart?"
The silence presses heavy between us. I want to answer,
to explain, but everything feels tangled, wrong, as if the
truth might break us more than the distance.
His eyes search mine, desperate for something a
reason, a hope, anything at all.
And I stand there, frozen, wondering if love is enough
to close the gap we both let grow.

"I feel it too," I whisper, finally breaking the quiet.
"We fit, perfectly like the world made us for this
moment."

His breath catches, hope flickering in his eyes, but I look away, because what comes next will hurt. "It's not about love," I say, my voice trembling.

"We have that. We've always had that. But love doesn't erase the timing, doesn't smooth out the jagged edges of our lives." He takes a step closer, his presence overwhelming. "Then why does it feel so right?" he asks, like the answer might somehow undo the truth.

"Because we are right," I admit, "but the world around us isn't. And we can't force it to be not yet."

His shoulders fall, the fire in him dimming, and it takes everything in me not to reach for him.

Not to let my heart override the quiet voice of reason that keeps us apart for something bigger. "I wish it could be now," I say, barely audible. As he nods, slowly, painfully, we both realize love isn't always enough to make the world align.

"But someday it will," I whisper, holding onto the thread of hope.
"We'll share the same cup, pour coffee into mornings we both built.
The same house, where walls hold our laughter,
And the silence feels like home instead of distance."

He looks at me, his eyes searching for certainty in my voice.
"Will we share the same thoughts," he asks
"not always the same words, but the same understanding.
The same rides windows down,
The world rushing past, and us moving forward."
He exhales slowly, his shoulders still heavy with the weight of now,
But I see it the faintest hint of a smile.
Because someday isn't just a hope anymore.
It's a promise waiting to be kept.

The winter I forgot to feel

The winter is back, shivering and cold,
Roses are gone, their stories untold.
Trees left dry, with branches bare,
A quiet ache fills the frosty air.

My mom is getting old, her steps now slow,
Her face reflects all the years that glow.
Like the branches that weather the storm,
She stands resilient, her heart still warm.

The winds may howl, the world may freeze,
But she's my shelter, my roots, my peace.
In her aging hands, a timeless grace,
A love that's eternal, no cold can erase.

The hands that never held me

My mom, lost in her book,
Turned two pages without a look.
A tiny mistake, so small, so slight,
Yet it felt like a flicker of light.

I watched and thought of all I've done,
Skipping moments, choosing to run.
From words unwritten, chapters untold,
Fears that lingered, dreams left cold.

How stupid, I think, to bear this pain,
To cry for rescue, call in vain.
But wait haven't I endured enough?
Scarred by time, yet playing tough.

I love perfumes and the coffee,
But the little girl wouldn't care, not really.
She was too busy giggling,
Lost in moments that weren't really there.

She laughed over a dad who couldn't see,
How deep her longing really could be.
Her heart was hidden behind each smile,
While she waited for him to stay awhile.

Her world was painted in shades of need,
Clinging to him, yet left to plead.
She didn't know the depth of the cost,
But I see how much was truly lost.

Lies kissex by your name

He asks for ten minutes of silence
After every storm we ignite,
But how do I breathe for ten seconds,
When the lipstick stains scream louder than the fight?

His eyes, once lanterns of my nights,
Now burn for a world where I don't belong.
I thought love would be our gentle song,
But the melody has faltered; I was wrong.

I built a world of "us" in fragile dreams,
Believing it would hold through shifting streams.
Yet here I stand, in silence I must bear,
As the truth unfolds in the stains he wears.

He smells like her, and he speaks for me,
But I know it's for her.
He might say he loves me,
But his sins speak louder.
I might have been simple and good,
But I am not enough to hold him.

I feel bad for her
If he can't love me for how much I have done for him,
He might not ever love her.

He might stay, but not stay.
He might hug, but not hold.
He might speak, but not listen.
He might buy her gifts, but never know her birthday.
He might lie, but never love.
He might promise, but never forever.
And he might never know her,
Yet still keep her trapped in his words.
And she might stay, thinking it's her forever,
But little does she know, it's the same river.
Things that are left are left for a reason,
For wisdom often comes after the season.

Dialects of the heart

People have different love languages,
And they ask me, "What's mine!?"
I don't have a long language
I mean, I am mean when I'm in love.

I'm crazy if I see her smile at your jokes,
Insane over the coffee you make,
Or the grin you've earned that's not mine to take.

Maybe I'll adore your curls,
Maybe I won't.
Maybe I'll love you entirely,
Or maybe I'll never.

My language isn't soft or kind,
It's reckless, raw, and undefined.
But if you read between my chaos and care,
You'll find my love is always there.

And I actually don't know what my love language is,
Because... how do people know what theirs is?
Is it from loving or from being loved,
From giving or from receiving,
Is it something we learn or just feel?

Maybe I'll never have the answer,
But you might be the answer,
Maybe more than that,
The question and the solution in one.

In your presence, I find pieces of things unsaid,
A truth that's not meant to be defined
Maybe love isn't a language at all,
But a feeling that echoes in the quiet moments,
In the way you make me forget
That there's ever a need for answers.

I love tulips, you love lilies,
Rain bothers me and gives you peace,
I take coffee without sugar,
While you can't get over your tea .

What the past couldn't carry

The lipstick was up,
But I capped it without twisting it down,
And it broke.

It fell to the ground,
And suddenly, I stopped
Am I like this too?
Quitting before things
Even reach the final line?

Stopping and always running before goodbyes,
Always insecure about the size or the price.
Never staying long enough to see how it could have felt,
Never sure if I was enough for it to last,
But always running,
Always questioning if I should've held on just a little longer.
Not because it was right or wrong,
But because I never let myself see it through.

Maybe it's not my fault,
Not my parents, not my friends,
Not those therapists who tried to fix me,
Maybe I was just born this way,
Or maybe it's the fear inside me,
A fear so deep it taught me to let go
Before I even touch the final line.

Tears of a love long gone

What breaks my heart, doesn't break yours,
What leaves me breathless, won't ever affect you,
What steals my air, will never flow through your veins.

What tears me apart, will never reach your soul,
What leaves me in shadows, will never darken your light,
What drowns me in silence, will never make you fall,
What breaks me inside, will never touch you at all.

My tears won't help, nor will the time,
But maybe if I just forget you,
Plant the strawberries I love,
And paint my nails blue,
Maybe then I won't remember you,
As the pain fades into the roots I have sown.

Better the Bear than a man

How am I suppose to speak for what's right

When my voice was never really mine

All I could do was barely breathe and they asked me to shine

But how can I when every breath feels like its not even mine

And they speak of femininity and they speak of womanhood, as if its some design

They shape it, they mould it they tell me its mine.

But its never been my truth

Just a label they assign.

They speak of fetal blood as if it's a sin to bear

As if it stains the earth something we are meant to foreswear
And then they ask why we choose the bear

A history written in Blood

Books scattered all around the room,
Though I know nothing, the only thing I try to hold is me.

So I will stop the manifest,
Since men go to wars and women bleed.
What's the point of dreams we keep,
When silence cuts and shadows weep?
The world divides, but pain is the same,
Carved in bodies, whispered in names.

Then God sits, and we find our knees glued to the ground,
We know nothing except our signs and sins we ran from.

We look into each other's eyes,
Hoping for someone to go first, but we can't
We don't want to.

The sky screams, and the birds die.
He asks, from a bird's eye,
"What do you do with your women, & why?"

Carving a blade to the bone

Growing up, I realized one thing:
Daughters who never tasted what
Calling a father her hero seems like,
Often are portrayed as selfish.
But since no Benefactor or Cherisher
 Comes for them,
They take a fair share of measuring love and distance.
Girls like those keep feathers in their books,
Saving every piece of things that fall apart.
They get shaped in the house of unemotional parents,
Who don't understand her urge to touch a butterfly,
And kiss her dad's cheek.
They're told to be strong, yet no one shows them how,
So they carry their softness in silence,
Worn but unbroken,
Longing for what was never taught to the
Tenderness, and the freedom to be fragile.
They are told to learn to keep their voices low,
And their eyes down,
But no one tells them it's fine to giggle loud
So they hide their scars, their heads bowed low,
What's the point of living, if they're never allowed to grow

The life without a line

What do you do when death is a step away,
And the future you built begins to sway?
Do you let it slide, like sand through hand,
Or mourn the one who drew the plan?
Do you recall the oceans wide,
The peacock's call, the rain outside?
Or do you summon the angels near,
To whisper peace against your fear?

Do you fear, or do you smile,
For it to take you for a while?
Do you wish to open your eyes,
To a world so bright, beyond the skies?

Where flowers don't dry and the smell of amber fills the sky?
Where the warmth stays constant, and the world is always fair.

The art of being enough

If someone breaks your heart,
Find the ugliest cup that catches no light,
Fill it with every note, every shard of their might.
When the rain comes, tip it gently aside,
Watch the steam curl upward, like ghosts in the tide.
Let the breeze hum secrets only it knows,
As the world turns softly and silently slows.
If you ever feel lost in the blur of the pain,
Run barefoot in the storm, through the puddles of rain.
Count the stares that linger, let them weigh down,
Wear them like whispers stitched into your crown.
Feel the ache sit quiet, like a bruise untold,
Because time is a thief, but it's clever and cold.
What's meant for you will never make you bow low,
It will come like a sunrise steady and slow.

The quite plea

We all know how things are never meant to stay,
Like fleeting feathers, connections drift away.
Yet, in the fleeting moments, we still dare,
To start something, fragile yet rare.
The trees know they'll lose their leaves to the cold,
As winter whispers its stories of old.
But still, they wait for spring to return,
Teaching us patience and how to yearn.
A whisper lingers, soft in the air,
"They don't stay because they're unaware.
They stay not because forever is near,
But because they're willing to face the fear."
And "together" never carried such weight,
A promise to face whatever fate.
Not bound by time, nor tethered by end,
But by the strength to stand and mend.

The Lost Chronicle

"Between the pages, I drown in silence and ink,
My hair caught in the breeze, but no one looks, no one thinks.
The texture of my skin, a canvas of time,
Etched with soft whispers, no rhythm, no rhyme.
The pearls on my neck, quiet yet strong,
A silent chorus that's lasted so long.
Womanhood sits like a poem, refined,
An artful balance of heart and mind.
I move like the breeze, unseen up slight,
An unspoken quietness, fading from sight.
Yet my hands hold stories, careful and small,
A mastery of grace in a world so tall.
Words stick to my throat, heavy and cold,
A story I live, but it's never been told."

Mend without peeling

When Storms Are Shared
When someone shares their storms with you,
I hope you don't compare; just see it through.
I hope you learn to bear the weight they hold,
And let their fears and truths unfold.
I hope you don't show how you're so apart,
Or remind them it isn't your fault to start.
Instead, stay near, their warmth, their guide
Hold them close as the waves collide.
If You Stay

Stay like swans, if forever's your aim,
Don't linger half-hearted, it's not a game.
If you must leave, then go before

The book of their scars is shown, and more.
Before their smile hides what's underneath,
The wounds, the storms, the quiet grief.
Don't open the pages just to walk away
Stay for the story, or don't start today.

The art of being patient

I met the fairy on my way home,
She stopped me there, said, "Why do you roam?"
I shrugged, "Just holding on, that's all.
It's like waiting for a door to crack open, but it doesn't fall."
She laughed, light as a breeze, "Don't you see?
Patience isn't waiting; it's the space between the plea."
I looked at her, couldn't quite make sense,
But all I felt was this weight, so dense.
"I'm holding," I said, "but it's not the same,
It's like you hold a rope, but it frays with the strain."
She nodded, "That's patience, love.
It's the tension in your grip, the thing you can't shove."
"Think of it like an oyster," she said with care,
"Patience is the shell, and the pearl's always there.
It's not about what you see, or what you find,
But the slow, steady work that happens behind."

"Inside it's quiet, and the world doesn't know.
A grain of sand, or a piece of hurt,
That's how the pearl begins, hidden in the dirt."
"Over time, it coats itself in layers,
Until it's something that can't be touched by prayers.
Not smooth at first, but rough in its shape,
It grows slowly, no promise of escape."

"I hope you find someone to share your coffee with, someone who understands the warmth of your mornings and the comfort in your silence. But if no one comes, I hope your taste only deepens with time, like the sea—beautiful on its own, even if there's no sky to reflect its depth."

The weight of goodby

How bad could a longing be
yeah, until you hide your tears beneath the blanket,
until the silence tastes like salt,
until your own breath feels like a weight you can't lift.
How bad could a goodbye go
until the last word loops like an old videotape,
worn, frayed at the edges,
but never quiet enough to forget.
How bad could moving on be
until you hate the last meal you shared,
until the taste turns to ash on your tongue,
until every familiar place feels like a wound reopening.
How bad could betrayal be
until your nails dig into your palms,
until you flinch at their name on your lips,
until trust itself feels like a lie you once believed.

The love from thousand years ago

Love doesn't come from empty promises;
it comes from the movement of breaking your nails
between your teeth,
those who break on the first day of being apart.
It comes from the days when the sun doesn't visit your window,
and those days when you hate your life and can't just fight.
It comes from the night you think of the fight,
yet nothing seems to go right.
It comes from the day you try to leave their sight,
but loving is the only thing you do right.

So is it right?
trying to fit and not let anything slip.
So is this what you wanted?
Is this the love you waited and prayed for?
Night walks and long talks
I see none but awkwardness
and empty words that could be filled,
but never for you.
Lie and say —no,
it's just because of the fight.

Maybe my mother was right
that love should never feel like waiting in the cold,
like holding out your hands for warmth
that never comes.
Maybe love was never meant to be
the silence between us,
the way my voice wavers
when I ask if you're still here,
or the way you answer
without ever really saying a thing.
Maybe love isn't the ache in my chest
when I watch you leave,
but the weight I carry
every time you come back.
Tell me, does love always mean
convincing yourself to stay?
To trade dreams for reality,
even when reality is nothing
but a slow unraveling?
Say it's just the way things go,
say we're not broken, just tired.
Say love is patience,
but patience was never meant
to outlive its own hope.
Maybe my mother was right.
Maybe love isn't supposed to feel
like something you have to survive.

www.ingramcontent.com/pod-product-compliance
Lightning Source LLC
LaVergne TN
LVHW061600070526
838199LV00077B/7125